I0810640

This book belongs to

and is a memento of
a very special day.

Written and compiled by Sophie Piper
Illustrations copyright © 2015 Lynn Horrabin

This edition copyright © 2015 Lion Hudson

The right of Lynn Horrabin to be identified as the illustrator of this work has been asserted by her in accordance with the Copyright, Designs and Patents Act 1988.

All rights reserved. No part of this publication may be reproduced or transmitted in any form or by any means, electronic or mechanical, including photocopy, recording, or any information storage and retrieval system, without permission in writing from the publisher.

Published by Lion Children's Books
an imprint of
**Lion Hudson plc**
Wilkinson House, Jordan Hill Road,
Oxford OX2 8DR, England
www.lionhudson.com/lionchildrens

ISBN 978 0 7459 6535 2 (blue)
ISBN 978 0 7459 6587 1 (pink)

First edition 2015

**Acknowledgments**
All unattributed prayers are by Sophie Piper and Lois Rock, copyright © Lion Hudson.
p. 4: John Newton (1725–1807)
p. 13: Mrs Cecil Frances Alexander (1818–95)
p. 22: Julia Carney (1823–1908)
p. 24: From a New England sampler
p. 46: Walter J. Mathams (1851–1931)
p. 48b: Victoria Tebbs, copyright © Lion Hudson
Bible extracts are taken or adapted from the Good News Bible © 1994 published by the Bible Societies/ HarperCollins Publishers Ltd UK, Good News Bible© American Bible Society 1966, 1971, 1976, 1992. Used with permission.
The Lord's Prayer (pp. 42–3) as it appears in *Common Worship: Services and Prayers for the Church of England* (Church House Publishing, 2000) is copyright © The English Language Liturgical Consultation and is reproduced by permission of the publisher.

A catalogue record for this book is available from the British Library

Printed and bound in China, December 2014, LH23

# My Baptism Album

*Written and compiled by* Sophie Piper
*Illustrated by* Lynn Horrabin

LION CHILDREN'S

May the grace of Christ our Saviour,
And the Father's boundless love,
With the Holy Spirit's favour,
Rest upon us from above.

*Eighteenth-century hymn*

Space for baby's photo

Some people brought their babies to Jesus for him to place his hands on them in blessing. The disciples saw them and scolded them for doing so, but Jesus called the children to him and said these words:

"Let the children come to me and do not stop them, because the kingdom of God belongs to such as these. Remember this! Whoever does not receive the kingdom of God like a child will never enter it."

From Luke 18:15–17

# About me

My name is

and I was born on

in a place called

The other people in my family are

# My family

Dear God, bless all my family,
As I tell you each name;
And please bless each one differently
For no one's quite the same.

In this
photo are

Space for a family photo

# My church family

One special day, my own little family introduced me to the much bigger church family.

Together, we can learn to live as Jesus taught, as his disciples.

Jesus said:

"Now I give you a new commandment: love one another. As I have loved you, so you must love one another. If you have love for one another, then everyone will know that you are my disciples."

Space for a photo of the church into which you were welcomed

# I learn about God

May all the world sing to our God!
The angels in the height,
the sun, the moon and silver stars
that glitter in the night;

The oceans and the giant whales,
the storms and wind and rain,
the animals and birds on every
mountain, hill and plain;

And all the people, young and old,
the wealthy and the poor:
sing praise to God who made the world,
sing praise for evermore.

From Psalm 148

All things bright and beautiful,
All creatures great and small,
All things wise and wonderful,
The Lord God made them all.

*A children's hymn*

# God loves me

Dear God,
I know I am only little.
I can't be in charge of big things.
But I know I am safe with God;
As safe as a baby in its mother's arms.

From Psalm 131

God feeds the birds that sing from the treetops;
God feeds the birds that wade by the sea;
God feeds the birds that dart through the meadows;
So will God take care of me?

God clothes the flowers that bloom on the hillside;
God clothes the blossom that hangs from the tree;
As God cares so much for the birds and the flowers
I know God will take care of me.

*Based on Matthew 6*

# God watches over me

Thank you, God in heaven,
For a day begun.
Thank you for the breezes,
Thank you for the sun.
For this time of gladness,
For our work and play,
Thank you, God in heaven,
For another day.

Traditional

Space for a photo of a happy day

# God guides me

Dear God,
Let me hear your voice
saying you are near
and will help me
through each day
so I need not fear.

Let me hear your voice,
dear God,
telling me the way
to goodness and
to gentleness
every single day.

*Based on Isaiah 30*

Thank you, God, for all the loving people who help me to grow up good.

Space for a photo of my parents

# A special message from

May my life shine
like a star in the night,
filling my world
with goodness and light.

From Philippians 2

Space for a photo of someone
who has promised to help me
grow up good

# A special message from

Little deeds of kindness,
Little words of love,
Help to make earth happy,
Like the heaven above.

*A child's hymn*

Space for a photo of someone
who has promised to help
me grow up good

# A special message from

God bless all those that I love;
God bless all those that love me;
God bless all those that love those that I love,
And all those that love those that love me.

*Traditional*

Space for a photo of someone
who has promised to help
me grow up good

# Prayers and promises from those who love me

# A counting prayer

This is my prayer number 1:
bless the day that's just begun.

This is my prayer number 2:
may the sky be clear and blue.

This is my prayer number 3:
God, please take good care of me.

This is my prayer number 4:
help me love you more and more.

This is my prayer number 5:
make me glad to be alive.

This is my prayer number 6:
help me when I'm in a fix.

This is my prayer number 7:
make this world a bit like heaven.

This is my prayer number 8:
put an end to hurt and hate.

This is my prayer number 9:
let the light of kindness shine.

This is my prayer number 10:
bring me safe to bed again.

# All about Jesus

When Jesus was born in Bethlehem, long ago, the angels sang.

Shepherds and wise men drew near in wonder.

When Jesus was a man, he told people about God's love.

He told them to follow his teaching and live as God's friends.

Then they would be part of God's kingdom.

I am little
I am lowly
God is great and
God is holy;
yet was born
a child like me
here on earth
for all to see;
came from heaven –
great and holy –
to a stable:
little, lowly.

# Jesus is born

The stars that shine at Christmas
Shine on throughout the year;
Jesus, born so long ago,
Still gathers with us here.
We listen to his stories,
We learn to say his prayer,
We follow in his footsteps
And learn to love and share.

Space for a picture of
my first Christmas

# What Jesus said

"Listen," said Jesus. "The only thing that really matters is being part of God's kingdom. Don't worry about anything else."

The kingdom of God
is like a tree
growing through
all eternity.

In its branches, birds may nest;
in its shade we all may rest.

Based on Matthew 13

## Fill in your family tree

# How to follow Jesus

Love the Lord your God more than anything: with all your heart, with all your mind, with all your soul, and with all your strength.

And love those near to you as much as you love yourself.

Let your life be like a light in a dark place: a life of good deeds that show the world God's love.

And that's important: your good deeds are to show the world about God, not for you to show off.

Love everyone: your friends, of course, and also those who are unkind to you.

Even when people treat you badly, be ready to forgive them.

And trust in God to bless you and take care of you.

From Luke 10 and Matthew 5, 6

# The good shepherd

"Listen," said Jesus. "God cares about everyone. It doesn't matter if they have forgotten to live as God wants.

"God is like a good shepherd. That shepherd may have a hundred sheep, but he cares deeply if even one goes missing.

"He goes and searches for his lost sheep. He does not stop looking until he finds it.

"And when anyone wanders far away from God, then God comes searching for them.

"When they return to the safety of God's love, all the angels sing."

Dear God, you are my shepherd,
You give me all I need,
You take me where the grass is green
And I can safely feed.

You take me where the water
Is quiet and cool and clear;
And there I rest and know I'm safe
For you are always near.

*Based on Psalm 23*

# Our Father

"When you pray," said Jesus,
"say these words:

"Our Father in heaven,
hallowed be your name,
your kingdom come,
your will be done,
on earth as in heaven.
Give us today our daily bread.
Forgive us our sins
as we forgive those who sin against us.
Lead us not into temptation
but deliver us from evil."

For the kingdom, the power,

and the glory are yours now and for ever. Amen.

# The Easter message

Jesus spoke of love. Others treated him cruelly. They had him put to death on a cross.

By God's power, he rose to life again.

The Easter message is that God's love is stronger than anything.

The autumn leaves fall to the earth,
In spring, the buds are green
and signs that God brings all to life
throughout the world are seen.

The Easter news of Jesus' life
shows death is not the end.
God's love will bring us safe to heaven
with Jesus as our friend.

# A friend of Jesus

Jesus, friend of little children,
Be a friend to me.
Take my hand, and ever keep me
close to thee.

*A children's hymn*

Space for a picture of me on the day of my baptism

# God is with me

God be with me, like a wind
that blows from heaven above:
may I be both bold and strong
to show the world your love.

God be with me, like a flame
that dances in the air:
may I bring the warmth of love
to people everywhere.

All glory to the Father,
All glory to the Son,
All glory to the Spirit:
God in three, yet one.

# Helping hands

May my hands be helping hands
For all that must be done
That fetch and carry, lift and hold
And make the hard jobs fun.

May my hands be clever hands
In all I make and do
With sand and dough and clay and things
Of paper, paint and glue.

May my hands be gentle hands
And may I never dare
To poke or prod or hurt or harm
But touch with love and care.

Space for a hand print.
Brush paint on the hand,
then press onto clean paper.
Make several and choose the best.

# Thank you for my home

Bless the window
Bless the door
Bless the ceiling
Bless the floor
Bless this place which is our home
Bless us as we go and come.

Space for a photo

# Thank you for my food

For health and strength
and daily food,
we praise your name,
O Lord.

*Traditional*

# Thank you for daytime

Thank you, God in heaven,
For a day begun.
Thank you for the breezes,
Thank you for the sun.
For this time of gladness,
For our work and play,
Thank you, God in heaven,
For another day.

*Traditional*

# Thank you for night-time

Day is done,
Gone the sun
From the lake,
From the hills,
From the sky.
Safely rest,
All is well!
God is nigh.

*Anonymous*

Space for a photo

When I lie down, I go to sleep in peace;
you alone, O Lord, keep me perfectly safe.

Psalm 4:8

# Thank you for a lifetime

Dear God,
May we sit down with friends through all our days:
On the plastic chairs of playgroup,
On the wooden chairs at school,
On the soft and sagging sofas of home,
On the folding chairs of holidays,
On the fashionable seats of restaurants
And on the dusty seats in the garden
Till at last, when we have grown old,
We need friends to help us in and out of chairs.

Space for a photo of me and some friends sitting together

# Thank you for my birthday

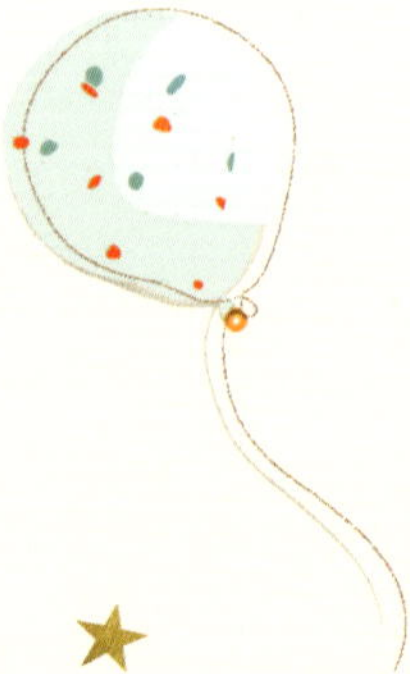

All around the seasons
another year has flown.
Now it is my birthday
and look how I have grown
all around the seasons
to celebrate this day
with everyone who loves me
and God to guide my way.

Space for a birthday photo

For blessings here
and those in store
we give thanks now
and evermore.